LIL BUB'S

LIL BOOK

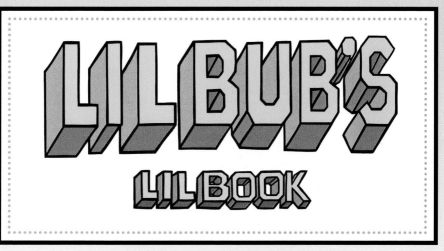

LIL BUB'S LIL BOOK

The **EXTRAORDINARY** Life
of the Most Amazing Cat **ON THE PLANET**

LIL BUB

GOTHAM BOOKS

GOTHAM BOOKS
Published by the Penguin Group
Penguin Group (USA) Inc., 375 Hudson Street,
New York, New York 10014, USA

USA | Canada | UK | Ireland | Australia | New Zealand | India | South Africa | China
Penguin Books Ltd, Registered Offices: 80 Strand, London WC2R 0RL, England
For more information about the Penguin Group visit penguin.com.

LIBRARY OF CONGRESS CATALOGING-IN-PUBLICATION DATA
Bridavsky, Mike.
  Lil Bub's lil book : the extraordinary life of the most amazing cat on the planet / [written by Mike Bridavsky].
  ISBN 978-1-592-40850-4 (pbk.)
  1. Cats—Humor. I. Title. II. Title: Lil book.
  PN6231.C23B75 2013
  818'.602—dc23   2013006114

Printed in the United States of America
10 9 8 7 6 5 4 3 2 1

Set in Janson Text and Champion • Designed by Spring Hoteling

While the author has made every effort to provide accurate telephone numbers, Internet addresses, and other
contact information at the time of publication, neither the publisher nor the author assumes any responsibility for
errors or for changes that occur after publication. Further, the publisher does not have any control over and does
not assume any responsibility for author or third-party websites or their content.

This book is
dedicated to
YOU.

My name is Mike, and I'm a relatively normal dude living in Bloomington, Indiana. I am also the caretaker, housemate, and number one pal of Lil BUB (although I just call her BUB).

In the summer of 2011, my friend's mother, Lori, rescued BUB when she discovered her as the runt of an otherwise healthy litter of feral kittens. Born with a multitude of genetic anomalies, BUB was quite different from her siblings and would require special attention and a permanent home. Since I am the owner of four other rescue cats, my friends immediately thought of me and sent me a picture of the most amazing creature I had ever seen. She looked like Gizmo from *Gremlins*, only cuter, and *real*. Naturally, I rushed over to meet her. When I picked her up, she looked me directly in the eyes and said *squonk*, to which I replied, "Hey, BUB." And that's how she got her name.

She was eight weeks old and weighed six ounces, which is alarmingly small, even for a kitten. My vet warned me that animals with BUB's types of birth defects often live only several months and may require a lot of medical attention. But after spending ten minutes with her sitting on my chest, purring like a motorboat, I knew I would do anything to help this remarkable critter. BUB does need more attention than a typical cat, but she repays me tenfold with affection, gratitude, beard cleanings, and unconditional love.

Now, at two years old, BUB is fully grown at four pounds, lives a happy and healthy life in my care, and is one of the most famous cats on the planet. BUB's rise to fame was completely unexpected and unplanned. It all started when a Web-savvy, cat-loving friend convinced me to share BUB's pictures on an online blog. In a matter of months, BUB was answering fan mail from devoted fans all over the world. It was then that it became clear to me that BUB is more than just a cute cat with a unique appearance. Her positive attitude, confidence, and perseverance are a source of inspiration to her fans, while her distinctive look demonstrates that being different is great. Rather than letting her fame become a flash in the pan, BUB treated it as an opportunity to do something important. Ever since, she has made it her priority to raise money for animal charities and to spread awareness about spaying, neutering, and rescuing and adopting pets. Her mission is to show how important it is to be compassionate toward those who are born different from the rest of us. As you enjoy this book, we hope it inspires you and others to appreciate everyone's differences—and maybe even adopt and take care of a special pet of your own.

Good job, BUB.

Hey, it's me, BUB. I am the most amazing creature on the planet. More specifically, I am a very special, one-of-a-kind cat. Some think I am actually from another planet. While this may or may not be true (it is), what is absolutely certain is that I bring hundreds of thousands of people great joy through images and videos of my amazing face and body. My limitless wisdom and razor-sharp wit paired with my ability to overcome disabilities provide laughter, hope, and inspiration to humans all over the world.

Please understand that I was not bred to be this way; I am one of nature's happiest accidents. I was born with an extreme case of dwarfism, so my limbs are disproportionately small to my already-tiny frame. I weigh in at four pounds, my lower jaw is underdeveloped, and my teeth never grew in, causing my tongue to poke out 95 percent of the time. I have huge, wonder-filled green eyes that can send messages into space and meticulously explore the deepest reaches of your soul. I am also equipped with opposable thumbs and extra toes on every paw. As you can see, I truly am a magnificent and superior being.

This book—specifically written by me for you—will give you an exclusive glimpse into the remarkable and fascinating story of my life, told through stunning photos depicting my travels through space and adventures on Earth. As you are about to discover, you just made the best decision by picking up this book.

Now, let's start with some facts.

I am a girl,
and I am real.

Or if you are lucky, directly into your brain.

I am from the planet Bub Ub Bub.

They better have
fishes down there.

I guess I should
try to find
fishes.

With this dude, I can defy gravity.

Together, we can
find fishes?

I don't
see any
fishes
here.

Behold, as one of your greatest cities is dwarfed by my magnificence.

Let's get
out of here;
I'm tired.

This dude is all right.

And apparently I'm pretty famous.

This is me telepathically signing autographs.

This is me
winning
a staring
contest
with time.

This is me telling you to take me to the park.

I DON'T CARE.
We're going in.

NO
PETS

**If I keep totally still,
I won't move.**

Whoa. Check out those slides.

Orange.

Green.

Life.   The universe.

Mrrrrrrrp.

I wish I could whistle.

Pretty
impressive,
I know.

OK. Can I have fishes now?

**Because it is
incredible.**

Time for bed.

Cue dream
sequence.

**I'm pretty sure
my family built these.**

Look, I'm at
STONEHENGE.

Mrrrrrrrrp.

Watch it, pal.

You're funny-looking.

OK. We're cool.

Nope. Still don't like avocados.

I'd rather be singing right now.

Busted.

That was terrifying.

Today, I meet up with Smoosh.

He is an exceptional Earth cat.

Sometimes I
don't know what
to say to him.

Awkward silence . . .

That worked.

Thanks for
all the fishes.

BONUS
BUB

More Photos, Fan Art,
and the Many Faces of BUB

BUB is cosmically grateful for the love and support of her fans, from the crazy cat people to the rock 'n' rollers, tattooers, business execs, lovers, and even the haters. BUB loves you all.

DUDE'S
ACKNOWLEDGMENTS

Thanks to all of my friends and family who made this book possible. You have no idea how much I appreciate your time, dedication, and support. Some of you traveled from all over the country on one week's notice to build giant ants, avocados, and sets of alien planets, while others spent weeks taking pictures of my cat. Some of you spent countless sixteen-plus-hour days editing photos in a dimly lit room. Others brought me food, because I forgot to eat. And then there are those of you who canceled weekend plans to take even more pictures of my cat or took care of BUB while I was away. The best part of making this book was realizing how fortunate I am to have so many incredibly talented, open-minded, and generous friends and family. I'm sure you know who you are, and I hope you know how much I love you.

Most of all I'd like to thank BUB. Thanks for choosing me to take care of you.

CREDITS

SET DESIGNERS: Pete Schreiner, Mark Rice, Erin Tobey

GUEST APPEARANCES: Colonel Meow, Henri, le Chat Noir, Smoosh, Special Agent Dale Cooper, Oskar, Josie, Vivian

PHOTOGRAPHERS: Chris Glass, Carli Davidson, Mike Bridavsky, David J. Woodruff, William Winchester Claytor, Mark Pallman, Asya Palatova, Brittany Purlee, Vincent Edwards, Molly Biehn, Larkin Biehn, Nathan Vollmar

ARTISTS: Ketch Wher, Alan Crenshaw, Jordan Trendelman, Johannah O'Donnell, Jana Renee Ayars, Nole Schuyler, Nicole J. Georges, Jessica Parmenter, Benny Phanichkul, Caitlin Dituro, Lindsay VanDeWeghe, Jennifer M. Miller, Colin McClain

STUNT DOUBLE: BULB

BUB

would like to thank the pets of the people who made this book
AMAZING.

Anne Clemmer, Asya Palatova, Carli Davidson, Chris Glass, Erin Tobey, Jonathan Cargill, Katherine Latshaw, Mark Rice, Mike Bridavsky, Nate Powell, Pete Schreiner, Julie Kraisler, William Winchester Claytor, LeeAnn Pemberton, Sophia Muthuraj, Erica Ferguson, Andrea Santoro, Susan Schwartz, Spring Hoteling, Rebecca Harris, William Shinker, Monica Benalcazar, Sandra Chiu, and Beth Parker.